HINTS

TO

YOUNG MINISTERS:

designed more particularly for

THE USE OF THOSE EDUCATED

AT

HOXTON ACADEMY.

By T. W.

London:

PRINTED BY W. SMITH, NO. 49, KING STREET, SEVEN DIALS.

1802.

HINTS, &c.

BRETHREN,

Suffer the word of exhortation,

MINISTERS are set upon a hill, as the lights of the world; and they are the salt of the earth: the vows of God are upon them. " The lips of the priests should keep knowledge ;" but if they corrupt the covenant of Levi, and betray the important trust, they will become contemptible and base before all the people. —They are the stewards of the mysteries of God; and " it is required in stewards that a man be found faithful."—See that ye be *real* christians yourselves.—Your work requires the greatest diligence and the most constant application.—Give attendance to reading, to exhortation, to doctrine; meditate on these things ; " give yourselves wholly to them." The indolent preacher is as an hireling, and not a shepherd.—Prepare your sermons as if all depended upon the means; and when you deliver them still depend upon the blessed Spirit as if you had made no preparation, for " the Apostles spake as the Spirit gave them utterance." Do not commit to memory more than the leading ideas of the subject: *words* will make haste to follow *things*.—Engage your heart as well as lips for the service of the sanctuary.—The best preparation for pulpit exercises is to understand the subject; the best rule for delivering what you have prepared, to feel it.—You preach not merely to explain God's word, but to save souls.—Never take a text which you do not understand; and make a point of conscience to give the literal meaning of it to the people, from whence the spiritual meaning must be drawn.—Improve occurrences; and on all occasional sermons, select the most striking and important subjects.—Never take a text which out of its proper connection can mean nothing. —Always keep to the truths in the text; and divide it in the plainest way.—Be cautious of too much dividing, and subdividing; let your ideas be well illustrated, and closely applied. When you have proved the truth of the principles you have laid down, you have done but little; it is from this point that you are to set out by a faithful application of them to the hearts of your auditory, to strip the sinner of every subterfuge and excuse, that conviction may lead to repentance. To produce this effect, leave your proofs and divisions behind, and address yourself to the conscience in powerful interrogatives.—A well-written letter is of no use unless properly directed; David was insensible till Nathan said " Thou art the man."

Do not presume that the majority of your congregations are believers; and beware of prophesying smooth things to please any one.—Take nothing for granted, but explain frequently what sin is, the nature of God, and the purity and extent of the law, that the gospel may appear in its full lustre— Ever keep first principles in view, viz.

RUIN, REDEMPTION, REGENERATION, exhibiting them under a variety of forms and metaphors. Music has only seven notes, but they form a variety without bounds and without end.—You cannot enlarge too frequently, on the miserable, desperate, and helpless condition of *all* men as sinners, both by nature and practice; nor insist too much on the necessity of being born again of the Spirit, and made new creatures in Christ Jesus; nor declare too often that justification is freely by God's grace, through the redemption that is in Christ Jesus. Set Christ forth as the " all and in all," as " the chief among ten thousand, the altogether lovely," as " the Wonderful, Counsellor, the Mighty God, the Everlasting Father, the Prince of Peace;" exalt and magnify him in his offices of Prophet, Priest, and King, and " preach not yourselves but Jesus Christ the Lord."—Take heed to your doctrine, for ye are the " watchmen who are set upon the walls of Jerusalem." Your hearers will consist of two sorts, believers and unbelievers: Believers again may be classed into babes, young men, and fathers: give to each a portion in due season.—Preach evangelical truths practically, and practical truths evangelically; and like a wise master builder lay a good foundation before you build thereon, and in every discourse keep in view DOCTRINE, EXPERIENCE, PRACTICE.

Bishop USHER said it will require all our learning to make things plain. Christ was a plain preacher; " without a parable spake he not unto them." " The common people heard him gladly." " The poor have the gospel preached unto them."—Mr. HERVEY made it a rule when preaching, always to speak so that the most illiterate could understand, and then he was sure others could. Dr. MANTON once preached before the Lord Mayor, and was heard with admiration by the more refined part of the audience; as he was returning home, a poor man pulled him by the sleeve, and said, " Sir, I was in hopes of " getting some good by your sermon, but I was much " disappointed, for a great deal of what you said I could " not understand, you were quite above me ;" the doctor, with tears in his eyes, returned the following answer, " My friend, if I did not give you a suitable sermon, you " have given me one, and by the grace of God, I will " never play the fool again to please the greatest or the " most polite audience in the world."—That is the best preaching which does most good.—The great touchstone in religion are the *affections:* fire may be painted, but the heat cannot.

Never attempt to copy the peculiar manner of other ministers; but speak in a natural, easy, affectionate, and persuasive way, suited to the place and people. Vary your voice; begin to speak about the middle key that you may rise and fall as occasion requires; but take care that you do not drop it at the end of a sentence, so that those at the farthest distance cannot hear.—Remember you must speak with *animation*, that the people may perceive you feel the subject, for without *energy* you are not likely to secure their attention, or to have many hearers.—Zeal without meekness is like a ship at sea in a storm, and meekness without zeal is like a ship at sea in a calm.—Mankind are sunk into so fatal a degeneracy, and are by nature at such an awful distance from God, and from all which is holy and happy, that all the earnest zeal of the preacher should be employed to shew them their danger, and point to the remedy.—Urge

what you deliver as a man would plead for his own life, and as if it were your last sermon.—Tell those who would have you spare yourself, that time is short, eternity is at hand, the judge is before the door.—If you partake of a portion of that Spirit which God gave without measure to his Son, you will speak with authority; and when you feel these special gracious influences on your heart, it will wonderfully assist you to declare the whole counsel of God.——Mr. DAVIES, of America, said, " perhaps once in three or four months,
" I preach in some measure as I could wish; that is, I
" preach as in the sight of God, as if I were to step from
" the pulpit to the supreme tribunal; I feel my subject, I
" melt with tears, or I shudder with horror, when I de-
" nounce the terrors of the Lord; I glow, I soar in
" sacred ecstasies when the love of Jesus is my theme;
" and, as Mr. BAXTER was wont to express it, I preach
" as if I ne'er should preach again, and as a dying man
" to dying men."

The ministerial commission is to preach the gospel to every creature; if men are in a sinful, miserable, lost condition, that is all the qualification necessary for making an offer of Christ to them.—Dr. GROVENOR on Luke xxiv. 47. says, It is very affecting, that the first offers of grace should be made to those who of all people in the world had done it the most despite; Christ commanded his apostles to " *Begin at Jerusalem*," tell them " I live, and because I am alive again, my death
" shall not be their damnation, nor is my murder
" an unpardonable sin. Tell them you have seen the
" prints of the nails upon my hands and feet, and the

" wounds of the spear in my side, and that those
" marks of their cruelty are so far from giving me
" vindictive thoughts, that every wound they have
" given me speaks in their behalf, pleads with the
" Father for the remission of their sins, and enables
" me to bestow it. By these wounds court and per-
" suade them to receive the salvation they have procur-
" ed. Nay, if you meet that poor wretch that thrust
" the spear into my side, tell him there is another
" way, a better way of coming at my heart, even my
" heart's love, if he will repent, and look upon him
" whom he has pierced, and mourn."—Man's inability
is voluntary, and therefore criminal and punishable.

Although we are not under the law as a *covenant*,
but under grace, yet it still remains as a touchstone of
the evidence of our love and obedience to Jesus as King
in Zion.—Detect and expose therefore that doctrine
which recognizes the Saviour as a prophet to teach, and
a priest to atone, but rejects him in his kingly office.
Although Jesus is the end of the law for RIGHTEOUS-
NESS to every one that *believeth*, yet love is the fulfilling
of the law, and true faith worketh by love, so that we
are not without law to God, " but under the law to
Christ." " Do we then make void the law through
faith? God forbid; yea, we establish the law."—Oppose
error by preaching up the truth in love, " for the wrath
of man worketh not the righteousness of God."—Never
mention the names of sects in the pulpit.—In a general
way use the doctrine of election as you use sugar in
your tea, which sweetens all, yet is not exclusively
seen.—We never venture our life, health, or limbs,

upon God's decrees, and why should salvation be expected but in the use of appointed means—Our duty lies both in a confidence in the Lord's power and a diligent attention to the whole of his revealed will.—Avoid personality.—Don't pray nor preach too long, but give the people much in a little; if you use ten words when five would do you may puzzle and confound.—As God has instituted in his church the membership of infants, and admitted them to it by a religious rite, baptize publicly as much as possible.—A declension of religion in a congregation generally begins in the pulpit: the distance between the first sinful indulgence, and the perfection of apostacy is not very remote. Both the lusts of the flesh, and the lusts of the mind, must be continually opposed and mortified.—Walk closely with God, and let the conversion of sinners lay near your heart.—He is generally found to be the most useful preacher who keeps most in his closet: go from your knees to the chapel.—Read the Word of God regularly through at least once in the year; all other books are cisterns, which can hold no more than what is put in them; why then should you be satisfying your thirst from the streams whilst the fountain is free of access? why content to sip when you are thus invited by the Lord, " Open your mouth, and I will fill it?" In the one you find only standing water, whilst the other is running or living water. And let me beseech you never to read the scriptures without previous fervent prayer to the Holy Spirit, to open your understanding, to understand them.— Become *thoroughly acquainted* with the bible: the doctrinal, experimental, and practical parts, may be compared to the head, heart, and members of the body; if separated, christianity appears a monster.

Take heed to your temper and spirit; for if the *fruit* of the Spirit is wanting in your habitual deportment, it is a sure evidence that you are destitute of the influences of the Spirit, and " if any man have not the Spirit of Christ he is none of his. The fruit of the Spirit is *love*." If therefore you are destitute of love, although possessed of every other gift, you are nothing.—" I " beseech you by the meekness and gentleness of Christ, " that as the servant of the Lord, you do not strive, " but be gentle unto all men, apt to teach, patient, in " meekness instructing those that oppose themselves, " if God peradventure will give them repentance to " the acknowledgment of the truth."—A good temper must be cultivated.—It is ill judged, though very common, to be less ashamed of a want of temper than understanding.—A congregation will not only adopt a minister's sentiments, but his very expressions and manner; hence the importance of temper as well as truth.—The very essence and beauty of christianity lies in having the same mind in us that was in Christ Jesus, and in conformity to that most lovely person, whose zeal for God's house eat up himself indeed, but did not devour those about him.—It is the second word or blow that makes the quarrel.—Forgive others every thing, and yourself nothing.—The surest way to keep others in temper, is to keep yourself so.—Never decide, resolve, nor act hastily, but take time for cool deliberation; and be quick to retract, instead of eager to defend a mistake—Make it appear, that it is no hard task for you to pronounce those little words, *I was mistaken*—Be not so ready to charge ignorance, prejudice, and mistake upon others, as you are to suspect yourself of them—A meek and quiet spirit is an unfading beauty, and an undecaying ornament: it is of " great price " in the sight of God."

The want of prudence will cloud the brightest talents, and eclipse the greatest gifts—" I wisdom *dwell* with prudence": The ground work of prudence must be laid in humility, meekness, and patience.—Condescend to all, but be familiar with few, for too much familiarity breeds contempt.—Tell your secret trials and temptations to very few.—Keep up the dignity belonging to the ministerial office: like the apostle Paul magnify your office.—" Be wise as the serpent, but harmless as the dove."—" Be swift to hear but slow to speak."—Stoop to the weakness and infirmities of your people, and take no notice of little things among them. He is not to be trusted who takes offence at trifles.—Beware of hasty friendships.—Never trust to appearances.—Avoid all useless controversies. Give up every thing for peace except truth.—Study human nature.—Whenever you reprove let it be tenderly, privately, and with all humility.—Make it a constant rule to pray for all who affront or injure you.—Be not elated at popularity, for those who are ready to pluck out their own eyes for you, will be the first to cry out, " away with such a fellow from the earth."—Recollect that every situation has its peculiar trials and difficulties.—Troubles are calculated to draw the heart nearer God, and to fit ministers for greater

Let your visits be short and spiritual; take care not to fall into the mischievous though common practice of gossiping; above all avoid " Levity, foolish talking, or jesting, which are not convenient."—Go out as little as possible to eat and drink.—Study good manners and affability in your behaviour, tempered with gravity; be always cheerful as well as serious, that you may win men to Christianity.—Visit the poor and the sick, and encourage a fund among your people to relieve the afflicted.—Exhort from house to house, and disperse religious tracts.—Seek opportunities of talking with the ungodly on the state of their souls, which will better qualify you in public to expose their delusions, and inform their minds; and by conversing with awakened consciences, you will be acquainted with the methods which the Holy Spirit takes, in the conversion of sinners unto God.

Carry the gospel into adjacent towns and villages, where men are perishing for lack of knowledge.—Although (says Mr. EWING) all the synagogues in the country were open to our Saviour, yet the wilderness, the river side, the sea shore, the mountain, the corn fields, the highway, the villages of Galilee, the streets of Jerusalem, and the porch of the temple, were all honoured, as places where Jesus condescended to preach the kingdom of heaven. Even in the most enlightened countries a vast body of people from their infancy are utter strangers to the house of God; but if you would cast yourself in their way, if you would carry the gospel to them (though no doubt busied in other pursuits) the prophecy would again be fulfilled, " the people which

sat in darkness saw a great light." The will of Christ
is indisputable; " Go out quickly into the streets and
" lanes of the city, and bring hither the poor, and the
" maimed, and the halt, and the blind; go out into the
" highways and hedges, and *compel* them to come in that
" my house may be filled." No other kind of preaching
has so immediate a tendency to enlarge the mind, and
to excite compassion and zeal. You will thus get
acquainted with the habits of thinking and practice
peculiar to every class, and learn to speak to every man
in his own way. Your private conversation, and public discourses, instead of being stiff, uninteresting, and
common-place remark, borrowed from books, or ex-
cogitated in the cloister, will come directly to the wants,
the convictions, the desires, and the prospects of those to
whom they are addressed.—Make occasional exchanges
with lively useful ministers. Religion will not flourish
without harmony and friendship with other ministers.
Associations formed to promote and extend vital godli-
ness in different counties are well calculated to carry
the important object into effect.—The doctrines of repentance towards God, faith in our Lord Jesus Christ,
and universal holiness, will employ your best and
brightest hours; while the gestures, the vestures, and the
fringes of religion, will be regarded no further than as
they have a plain and evident connection with faith and
love, with holiness and peace.—In the Redeemer's
catholic kingdom " there is neither Jew nor Greek,
" circumcision nor uncircumcision, Barbarian, Scy-
" thian, bond nor free, but Christ is all and in all."—
In a bed of tulips scarce any two are exactly alike.—

Love all without exception that have any thing of the image of Christ upon them.

Pay particular regard to youth by promoting Sunday schools and religious instruction. The children of the present age (says Dr. WATTS) are the hope of the age to come; the circle of thirty years will plant another generation in our room; another set of mortals will be the chief actors in the greater and less affairs of this life, and will fill the world with blessings or with mischiefs. If you have any concern for the glory of God in the rising generation, any solicitude for the propagation of virtue and happiness, to those who shall stand up in our stead; hearken to the voice of God, " Train up a child in the way he should go, and when he is old, he will not depart from it."—Catechising will be a mean to fit ministers to preach, and it will enable others to hear them with greater advantage.—Talk familiarly to children about religion; put easy questions to them; * encourage them occasionally by some little presents. Select some of the most promising from your Sunday school to learn writing and accounts, and promote a school of industry for female children, who in many places are in the most wretched circumstances for want of employment.

Where the gospel has its full influence, it calls forth into exertion, all the powers of the soul; and pro-duces the most tender concern for the happiness of

* See An easy Explanation of the Assembly's Catechism, requiring no other reply to short and plain questions than Yes or No, lately published by the Rev. GEORGE BURDER.

mankind. This concern does not evaporate in unavailing pity, but rouses to action, and girding itself for service, inquires, " What can be done toward banishing human misery, and making man happy?" Shall the mechanic, the manufacturer, the artist, and the philosopher, be all actively employed, with the utmost stretch of thought, to find out what may be useful in their peculiar arts and sciences; while the professed Ministers of Jesus, employ no energies, nor exert the vigour of their souls in *their* proper department? Let it rather appear that you are busied in discovering every way of access for divine truth to the human heart, and that you are resolved to employ every means you can think of, as conducive to that end.—Your reward does not depend on your success, but on your labor.

Be like a dead man to the world; both to its pleasures, vanities, and governing principles, and enforce the same upon others: " If any man love the world the love of the Father is not in him,"—True respectability consists in holiness, love, and growth in grace—Simplicity and godly sincerity do wonders. Beware of self-conceit. You must be emptied of self in every form, and become poor in spirit, less than the least of all saints, nay the very chief of sinners in your own sight. The devil's master-piece is to make us think well of ourselves.—A minister of Christ must exercise self-denial, and know how to bear hardship, suffering, and contempt.— Young Joseph, like other young men, dreamt about others bowing down to him, he never dreamt about going to prison.—Lay *yourself* in the dust, and none else can put you there; for only by pride cometh contention: Before honor is humility. The Holy Spirit, like water, always seeks the lowest place.

Shew no marked attention to any young woman, unless you design the honorable connection of marriage; and that person only is suitable who is converted to God, and whose education has qualified her to conduct herself with great prudence and economy: seek happiness before riches, goodness before greatness.—Rise early, spend your evenings at home, and don't sit up late.—Avoid the habit of smoaking, and the use of spirituous liquors—Live in a plain frugal way; " Owe no man any thing but love." Always appear neat and clean, but not foppish. Give the family where you reside as little trouble as possible; never desire any of them to do any thing for you that you can conveniently do for yourself.—Observe rule and order in every thing, and always begin public worship at the exact time.—Never engage in political disputes; pray for the king, and those in authority, " that we may lead quiet and peaceable lives."

PREACH WELL—LIVE WELL—RULE WELL.

" A bishop must be blameless as the steward of God,
" not self-willed, not soon angry, not given to wine,
" no striker, not given to filthy lucre: But a lover of
" hospitality, a lover of good men; sober, just, holy,
" temperate; ruling well his own house, holding fast
" the faithful word; that he may be able by sound
" doctrine both to exhort and convince gainsayers."

FINIS.

Smith, Printer,
King-Street, Seven-Dials.

www.ingramcontent.com/pod-product-compliance
Lightning Source LLC
Chambersburg PA
CBHW081455070426
42452CB00042B/2740